LOOKING INTO THE PAST:
PEOPLE, PLACES, AND CUSTOMS

Santas of the World

by

George Ouwendijk

Chelsea House Publishers

CHELSEA HOUSE PUBLISHERS
Editor-in-Chief Stephen Reginald
Managing Editor James D. Gallagher
Production Manager Pamela Loos
Art Director Sara Davis
Picture Editor Judy Hasday
Senior Production Editor Lisa Chippendale
Designer Takeshi Takahashi

First Printing

1 3 5 7 9 8 6 4 2

Library of Congress Cataloging-in-Publication Data

Ouwendijk, George.
Santas from around the world / by George Ouwendijk.

    p. cm. — (Looking into the past)
Includes bibliographical references and index.
Summary: Explains that people of various cultures form
around the world have different ideas about Santa Claus or a
comparable mythical figure who is often seen as a gift-giver.

ISBN 0-7190-4678-8

1. Santa Claus—Juvenile literature. [1. Santa Claus.]
I. Title. II. Series.
GT4992.O89 1997
398_.352—dc21   97-26802
                                                    CIP
                                                    AC

CONTENTS

CULTURE, CUSTOMS, AND RITUALS

T he important moments of our lives—from birth through puberty, aging, and death—are made more meaningful by culture, customs, and rituals. But what is culture? The word *culture,* broadly defined, includes the way of life of an entire society. This encompasses customs, rituals, codes of manners, dress, languages, norms of behavior, and systems of beliefs. Individuals are both acted on by and react to a culture—and so generate new cultural forms and customs.

What is custom? Custom refers to accepted social practices that separate one cultural group from another. Every culture contains basic customs, often known as rites of transition or passage. These rites, or ceremonies, occur at different stages of life, from birth to death, and are sometimes religious in nature. In all cultures of the world today, a new baby is greeted and welcomed into its family through ceremony. Some ceremonies, such as the bar mitzvah, a religious initiation for teenage Jewish boys, mark the transition from childhood to adulthood. Marriage also is usually celebrated by a ritual of some sort. Death is another rite of transition. All known cultures contain beliefs about life after death, and all observe funeral rites and mourning customs.

What is a ritual? What is a rite? These terms are used interchangeably to describe a ceremony associated with a custom. The English ritual of shaking hands in greeting, for example, has become part of that culture. The washing of one's hands could be considered a ritual which helps a person achieve an accepted level of cleanliness—a requirement of the cultural beliefs that person holds.

The books in this series, *Looking into the Past: People,*

Places, and Customs, explore many of the most interesting rituals of different cultures through time. For example, did you know that in the year A.D. 1075 William the Conqueror ordered that a "Couvre feu" bell be rung at sunset in each town and city of England, as a signal to put out all fires? Because homes were made of wood and had thatched roofs, the bell served as a precaution against house fires. Today, this custom is no longer observed as it was 900 years ago, but the modern word *curfew* derives from its practice.

Another ritual that dates from centuries long past is the Japanese Samurai Festival. This colorful celebration commemorates the feats of the ancient samurai warriors who ruled the country hundreds of years ago. Japanese citizens dress in costumes, and direct descendants of warriors wear samurai swords during the festival. The making of these swords actually is a separate religious rite in itself.

Different cultures develop different customs. For example, people of different nations have developed various interesting ways to greet each other. In China 100 years ago, the ordinary salutation was a ceremonious, but not deep, bow, with the greeting "Kin t'ien ni hao ma?" (Are you well today?). During the same era, citizens of the Indian Ocean island nation Ceylon (now called Sri Lanka) greeted each other by placing their palms together with the fingers extended. When greeting a person of higher social rank, the hands were held in front of the forehead and the head was inclined.

Some symbols and rituals rooted in ancient beliefs are common to several cultures. For example, in China, Japan, and many of the countries of the East, a tortoise is a symbol of protection from black magic, while fish have represented fertility, new life, and prosperity since the beginnings of human civilization. Other ancient fertility symbols have been incorporated into religions we still practice today, and so these ancient beliefs remain a part of our civilization. A more recent belief, the legend of Santa Claus, is the story of a kind benefactor who brings gifts to the good children of the world. This story appears in the lore of nearly every nation. Each country developed its own variation on the legend and each celebrates Santa's arrival in a different way.

New rituals are being created all the time. On April 21, 1997, for example, the cremated remains of 24 people were launched into orbit around Earth on a Pegasus rocket. Included among the group whose ashes now head toward their "final frontier" are Gene Roddenberry, creator of the television series *Star Trek,* and Timothy Leary, a countercultural icon of the 1960s. Each person's remains were placed in a separate aluminum capsule engraved with the person's name and a commemorative phrase. The remains will orbit the Earth every 90 minutes for two to ten years. When the rocket does re-enter Earth's atmosphere, it will burn up with a great burst of light. This first-time ritual could become an accepted rite of passage, a custom in our culture that would supplant the current ceremonies marking the transition between life and death.

Curiosity about different customs, rites, and rituals dates back to the mercantile Greeks of classical times. Herodotus (484–425 B.C.), known as the "Father of History," described Egyptian culture. The Roman historian Tacitus (A.D. 55–117) similarly wrote a lengthy account about the customs of the "modern" European barbarians. From the Greeks to Marco Polo, from Columbus to the Pacific voyages of Captain James Cook, cultural differences have fascinated the literate world. The books in the *Looking into the Past* series collect the most interesting customs from many cultures of the past and explain their origins, meanings, and relationship to the present day.

In the future, space travel may very well provide the impetus for new cultures, customs, and rituals, which will in turn enthrall and interest the peoples of future millennia.

Fred L. Israel
The City College of the City University of New York

CONTRIBUTORS

Senior Consulting Editor FRED L. ISRAEL is an award-winning historian. He received the Scribe's Award from the American Bar Association for his work on the Chelsea House series *The Justices of the United States Supreme Court*. A specialist in early American history, he was general editor for Chelsea's *1897 Sears Roebuck Catalog*. Dr. Israel has also worked in association with Dr. Arthur M. Schlesinger, jr. on many projects, including *The History of U.S. Presidential Elections* and *The History of U.S. Political Parties*. They are currently working together on the Chelsea House series *The World 100 Years Ago*, which looks at the traditions, customs, and cultures of many nations at the turn of the century.

GEORGE OUWENDIJK is a historian and educator at the City College of New York and the School of Visual Arts. His interests include the history of science, religious beliefs, and magic. After a lifetime of warm Christmases in Southern California, he now enjoys the brisk Yuletide Season of New York City.

The Legend of Santa Claus

Santa Claus is the favorite person of many of the world's children. Most of these children expect a jolly man who wears a red suit and delivers wonderful presents. But Santa Claus did not always exist. In fact, he is a fairly recent development. Nevertheless, the tradition of the "gift-giver" is one that many cultures share. One can say that Santa Claus, in one form or another, is a familiar figure to people the world over.

The modern figure of Santa Claus is a mixture of many historical and cultural traditions. The most ancient of these traditions is that of Saint Nicholas of Myra. St. Nicholas was born about A.D. 280 in Patara, which is located in the modern country of Turkey. Many miracles were attributed to this Christian saint during his lifetime, and these helped to create his reputation as a protector and helper of those in need. St. Nicholas, for example, is supposed to have saved sailors from drowning in a storm. For this reason, he became the patron saint of mariners, protecting them against storms and shipwreck. Now, St. Nicholas is also the patron saint of merchants, of the falsely accused, of endangered travelers, and of farmers.

One story about St. Nicholas was the basis for the modern legend of Santa Claus. St. Nicholas once gave gold to a man who was poor and had three unmarried daughters. With this act of charity, St. Nicholas made it possible for their father to pay for their dowries. In the society of that day, this meant that the daughters would marry into good families and be able to raise their children well. St. Nicholas threw a small pouch full of gold into the window of the man's house three different times, one for each daughter. He did not tell the man who he was, nor did he reveal his face. He remained an anonymous giver, just as the modern Santa Claus is never seen delivering gifts.

Many people have believed that Santa Claus, in the person of "Sintaklaas," came to America with the first Dutch settlers of New York, or New Amsterdam as New York City was then called. In reality, Santa Claus was the invention of 19th-century American writers and artists. When Dr. Clement Clarke Moore wrote a poem called *A Visit from St. Nicholas* for his own children in 1822, many people remembered old stories told about St. Nicholas. Santa Claus made his debut, carrying his sack of toys and riding in a reindeer-drawn flying sleigh, in the lines of this famous poem, which begins, "Twas the night before Christmas, when all through the house/Not a creature was stirring, not even a mouse...."

Forty years after Dr. Moore wrote about the night before Christmas, most Americans had heard the Dutch name for St. Nicholas, "Sintaklaas," but they mispronounced it as "Santa Claus," and so Santa got his name. In the 1860s, an artist named Thomas Nast began to draw pictures of Santa Claus for *Harper's Weekly* magazine. These drawings, with the plump, jolly man wearing a strange suit and full beard, became the basis for the way in which people have pictured Santa Claus ever since.

GERMANY

St. Nicholas traditionally brought gifts to German children on the eve of his feast day, December 6. He travelled with a frightening companion who carried wooden branches to scare children who acted badly or did not know their prayers during the year. This companion was most commonly known as Knecht Rupprecht, or "Servant Rupprecht." He was also known by other names such as Pelznickle, which means "Furry Nicholas," and Ru-Klas, which means "Rough Nicholas." These names hint that Knecht Rupprecht was more than just a companion for St. Nicholas. He was probably viewed as a meaner version of the kindly saint.

Religious changes in Germany have changed the relationship between the German people and St. Nicholas. As a result, St. Nicholas has come to resemble an American Santa Claus of the 20th century. He now often wears a red suit and white beard. Moreover, he is increasingly known as Father Christmas and appears more often on Christmas Eve rather than on his traditional feast day.

But the old traditions still remain in different parts of Germany. There are many names that are still used to refer to St. Nicholas and his companion, Knecht Rupprecht. In many areas one can still hear the names of Krampus, Pelzebock, or Gumphinkel used for Knecht Rupprecht. Elsewhere one hears Kläasbuur, Burklaus, Rauklas, Bullerkläas and Sunnercla as other names for St. Nicholas. And in the far east of the country, there exist more wild characters who substitute for St. Nicholas.

BELGIUM

elgium has two Santa Claus figures. St. Nicholas visits all the children of Belgian families who speak the Waloon language. In fact, St. Nicholas visits these homes twice, but this is not always as good as it sounds! He first comes on December 4 so he can find out which child has been good and which has been bad. Then St. Nicholas returns on December 6 bringing what each child deserves. To the good, he brings sweet candies and small toys. To the bad, he brings bunches of twigs. He leaves these in the children's shoes or in small baskets that are left just inside the doorway.

The other Santa Claus of Belgium is Père Noël. Père Noël visits the homes of French-speaking Belgians. When Père Noël visits, he usually brings his companion, Père Fouettard, who inquires about the behavior of each child. Obviously, Belgian children must behave well in order to receive the chocolates and candies that good children deserve. If not, they are likely to get a handful of sticks.

Both of these gift-givers visit on December 6, the feast of St. Nicholas. Christmas is a religious holiday in Belgium, and is observed with services in churches and quiet family gatherings. Special Christmas cakes are baked and served during the holiday season and are a treat for children and adults alike.

SWITZERLAND

Switzerland is a small country with many different traditions, and the Swiss have pulled together the Christmas lore of many different cultures. Consequently, they also have many Santas and gift-givers.

As in almost all Germanic cultures, the Swiss have always looked to St. Nicholas as a bringer of both gifts and prosperity. Elsewhere in Switzerland, children and adults may be visited by Father Christmas and his wife Lucy. Father Christmas resembles the French Père Noël, but he is accompanied by his friendly wife, not the unpleasant Père Fouettard who punishes unruly children in France. A married Santa figure is still rather unusual. Nevertheless, the Swiss seem to be very happy with this gift-giving couple. Perhaps they represent the traditional security and contentment that the Swiss have valued so much in their history.

Another gift-giver in Switzerland is the Christkind. Christkind means "Christ Child" and originally referred to the infant Jesus who was believed to bring Christmas gifts. The Christkind eventually became more like an angel who brings gifts instead of the Holy Child. Images of the Christkind show it as a childlike figure that shines with a bright, warm light. It has golden wings, and the Swiss often leave a window open so the Christkind can enter their homes. As the identity of the Christkind has changed over time from the infant Jesus to an angelic helper, its name has also changed. Christkind is sometimes called Kris Kringle. In the United States and several other countries, Kris Kringle is another name for Santa Claus. This is because a famous American movie, *Miracle on 34th Street,* was a Christmas story featuring a character named Kris Kringle.

AUSTRIA

ustria shares Christmas traditions with neighboring countries like Switzerland and Germany. Historically, St. Nicholas has arrived on his feast day, December 6, to bring the blessings of the season. And from the Middle Ages, the Three Wise Men have also made appearances on January 6 to the sounds of singing and cheerful processions. Gifts, however, have always been brought by the Christkind.

As in Switzerland, the Christkind originally was the infant Jesus who brought gifts to all children at the Christmas season. The Christkind is now an angelic being who is clothed in radiant light and has golden wings. It is a divine helper that delivers delicious chocolates to eager children. The Christkind usually announces the arrival of all the gifts by ringing a bell in Austrian homes.

The Christmas season sees several strange beings that have long wandered the Austrian forests. One is Krampus, who appeared in the earliest legends as a demon from the dark and wooded areas of Austria. He is now the companion of St. Nicholas. Krampus carries a wooden stick to punish children who have been bad or do not do their school lessons. But St. Nicholas has never let Krampus use his awful tool. Instead, children who quickly promise to be good and to study hard receive a reward from St. Nicholas and are spared the wrath of Krampus.

The first Christmas tree is believed to have been put up in Austria in the eighth century by English monks.

FRANCE

n France, Santa Claus is Père Noël, which means "Father Christmas." He does not appear until sometime after the late supper that the French people eat to celebrate Christmas, following their Midnight Mass on December 25. Once this delicious meal is finished, all the children line their shoes up near the fireplace. They hope that Père Noël can easily find them and fill them with candies and other treats. Traditionally, these shoes were "sabots," the wooden shoes of rural peasants. Today, however, any shoe will do as a convenient holder of sweets.

But Père Noël is only one of two gift-givers in France. There is also Petit Noël. This is the Christ Child, and this figure is similar to the Christkind found in Austria. Petit Noël brings gifts to the children that live in the parts of France that Père Noël does not usually visit. These Santa Claus figures of France have long been the most important parts of the French gift-giving tradition.

The religious aspects of Christmas have always been very important in France. The *crèche,* a nativity display which usually includes figures of the baby Jesus, Mary, Joseph, shepherds, and wise men in a stable, became popular in France hundreds of years ago. Parties are also held on the "Feast of the Kings," or Epiphany, in January, to close out the holiday season.

DENMARK

enmark is a Scandinavian country with a rich tradition of Christmas characters. Santa Claus, or Julemanden as the Danes call him, is now the main gift-giving individual in this country. Denmark only made its first official recognition of Santa Claus in 1958, when the Danes printed a portrait of Santa Claus on a Christmas seal. Santa Claus has become very popular since then, however, and his smiling face and red suit are now seen everywhere during the Christmas season. But the Danes do not believe that Santa Claus lives at the North Pole. He lives in Greenland which is, for all practical purposes, just like the cold and icy North Pole.

Denmark also has older Christmas traditions about gift-givers that are still very common. The Danish people warn children and visitors to beware of the Julnisser. These are elves that have always lived in barns and attics. They watch over animals and livestock during most of the year. The Julnisser wear gray woollen clothes and red caps, and on their feet are long red stockings and wooden clogs. The only creature that seems to be able to see them is the family cat. At Christmas time, these elves have been responsible for lost shoes, combs, and other things. They become practical jokers when Christmas arrives, doing mischievous things like blowing out the *Julebaal,* which is a Christmas fire that burns to drive away evil spirits. The only way to keep the Julnisser peaceful is to give them bowls of rice pudding. Fortunately, if the Julnisser are kept happy, they make sure that children and others find the occasional treat or lost coin.

FINLAND

inland is a very cold northern country. Christmas has always been associated here with winter, with sleighs drawn by horses, and with heavy coats. Many Finnish Christmas traditions have contributed to the beliefs about Santa Claus that are shared by other cultures.

In Finland, Santa Claus is known as *Joulupukki,* which means "Yule Buck." Joulupukki has presided over the Christmas season in Finland for many centuries. This season is celebrated by a popular tradition called the Feast of the End of Darkness, which marks the winter solstice and the very beginnings of spring and summer. Joulupukki began as a creature that did not give presents; instead, he demanded them. If he did not receive them, then he caused all sorts of mischevious problems. He might curdle milk or blow out cooking fires.

Joulupukki later changed into a friendly figure much more like the English Father Christmas and has now come to resemble a modern Santa Claus. But many of the old traditions still remain. Finnish children still believe that Joulupukki lives on *Korvatunturi,* which means "Mt. Ear." From there, he can hear the wishes of all Finnish children for Christmas treats and gifts. Joulupukki also needed many helpers to do all his work. There are many gnomes, or *tontut* as they are called in Finnish, that help Joulupukki make all the gifts and deliver them to the many children. Originally, these gnomes were very active throughout the year. Now they work mostly at Christmas time, but they still watch children from behind doors and under beds all year round to see if they misbehave.

NORWAY

orway is a Scandinavian country that did not simply adopt the modern figure of Santa Claus. It already had a centuries-old gift-giver tradition to draw upon.

It is Julesvenn who brings Christmas gifts to Norwegian children. In the past, Julesvenn always appeared as a friendly gnome or elf that brought barley stalks to homes during mid-winter feasts. He would hide these stalks in unlikely places, which forced children to find them in fun games of discovery. Julesvenn now brings many kinds of gifts to Norwegian children. He brings toys and treats, chocolates and sweets, and the children look forward to his coming just as children elsewhere look forward to Santa Claus.

Julesvenn is an old Christmas character in Norway, but so too are the many barn elves and Julebukk, the "Christmas buck." The barn elves of Norway are like those of Denmark. They must be fed rice pudding or else they will play practical jokes and cause many problems. Julebukk, an ancient character, is a little gnome or elf who brings gifts. He comes from the distant past when the Norwegians worshipped the god Thor and his goat. Today, the Norwegian Christmas includes a mixture of ancient customs with more modern ones. Modern Norwegian children "play" julebukk as a game like trick-or-treat. They dress up in costumes and go from door to door asking for gifts of candy and chocolate.

SWEDEN

hough the Swedes do not think of Santa Claus as many other people do, they have rich and ancient gift-giving traditions related to the Christmas season. The long Christmas season in Sweden, from December 13 to January 13, features many events that involve gift-giving. This season begins with St. Lucia's Day, which is named for a small child who was martyred in the year A.D. 304. On this day, the eldest daughter in the family wears a white dress with a red sash, and she wears an evergreen wreath with seven lighted candles on her head. She brings coffee, sweet buns, and cookies to her parents and the younger children while they are still in bed.

On Christmas Eve, everyone opens their gifts. These gifts were brought by a gnome called Jultomten who carries a huge sack on his back. The Jultomten is an ancient creature in Sweden and has long lived under the floors of homes and barns. He emerges on Christmas Eve to deliver his wonderful baggage while riding a Julbok, a straw goat that comes from ancient times. All of the presents have funny poems that hint at what is inside each box.

At the end of the Christmas season, on January 6, the Star Boys come out, carrying long poles with lighted stars. They sing Christmas carols as they stroll from house to house, and their Swedish neighbors give them many treats. At any time during the Christmas season, a Swede may receive a *Julklapp,* or "Christmas box." There will be a loud knock at the door, and a present will be thrown in. The giver hurries away without being recognized. The present will also be mysterious because it may be hidden in many boxes and fancy papers, or it may just contain instructions which tell where the real present can be found.

GREECE

t. Nicholas is very popular in Greece. He has always been an important religious figure, but over the years he has become more than that. At the launching of a boat, for example, there will probably not be a bottle of champagne broken across the new vessel's bow. Instead, a priest will bless a boat and ask for the protection of St. Nicholas as the patron saint of mariners. Traditionally, St. Nicholas wears clothes that are drenched with seawater. His face and beard drip with the sweat of his efforts to keep sailors safe when storms stir up the Mediterranean Sea.

Greece is one country where St. Nicholas shares attributes with other beings that resemble Santa Claus. These other beings are the *kallikantzaroi*, which are elves or sprites that only appear during the Christmas season. These are very ancient creatures that have always been a part of Greek culture. They emerge from the center of the earth and sneak into people's houses through chimneys. The kallikantzaroi are not evil, but unlike Santa Claus they are mischievous. They put out cooking fires, make milk go sour, and ride on people's backs and make them dance until they are exhausted.

In order to keep these trouble-makers out of their homes, the people of Greece keep their fireplaces burning during Christmas with a large log called a *skarkantzalos*. This is the traditional yule log of the Christmas season. The Greeks might also burn salt, or old shoes, the smell of which will keep the kallikantzaroi away. Greek children do receive gifts, but this usually occurs on St. Basil's Day, January 1.

RUSSIA

St. Nicholas has long been a very popular figure in Russia during the Christmas season. A legend exists about Prince Vladimir who went to Constantinople in the 11th century to be baptized. He was impressed by the deeds of St. Nicholas of Myra and brought home to Russia many stories of the saint's miracles and teachings. St. Nicholas was well loved in Russia, and many people have traditionally named their sons Nicholas after this beloved saint.

After the Russian Revolution of 1917, all religious figures were suppressed, including St. Nicholas. But the idea of St. Nicholas survived in the form of Grandfather Frost, who often resembles Santa Claus, although he tends to be thin and a little somber. Traditionally, Russians have had another figure who resembles Santa Claus. This was Kolyada, a name that means "Christmas." She was a white-robed young girl who went from house to house in a sleigh on Christmas Eve. She and her attendants would sing Christmas carols and receive small gifts and treats.

Russians also have a gift-giver called Babouschka who is much like the Italian La Befana. Babouschka means simply "grandmother." She is an old woman who refused food and shelter to the three wise men who traveled to Bethlehem to see the baby Jesus. Babouschka now travels the countryside looking for the wise men and brings gifts of food and treats to Russian children on January 5, the Eve of the Epiphany. Babouschka was also forgotten after the Russian Revolution, but with recent political change in Russia, stories about her are making a return.

HOLLAND

s do many other cultures, the Dutch recognize St. Nicholas as Santa Claus. St. Nicholas, or Sinterklaas as the Dutch call him, arrives at the end of November and establishes a headquarters to last him throughout the Christmas season. Sinterklaas wears the traditional and rather somber robes of a bishop of the church, and he has a servant named Black Peter who wears the colorful clothing of a 16th-century Spanish gentleman. Both Sinterklaas and Black Peter represent the struggles with Spain that the Dutch had in the 16th and 17th centuries.

Sinterklaas and Black Peter do not travel on a sleigh pulled by reindeer. They usually arrive in the Netherlands by ship in the main port of Amsterdam. The Dutch people come in great crowds to welcome him, thus making all normal city business come to a stop. Both of these figures are important and are greeted by the people of the city, including the mayor and other officials. They move at the head of a long procession to the Royal Palace, where they meet the royal family, especially the royal children. Each of the children must give an account of their behavior for the past year to Black Peter, just as all Dutch children must do.

Finally, on December 5, Dutch children receive their gifts, but this is itself an adventure. The presents are always called "surprises" because they are hidden throughout the house, and the children must discover each one. Sometimes, if they are small, these surprises are wrapped inside a huge box, or they are hidden inside a pudding or a vegetable! Large gifts may be hidden in cellars or attics with elaborate clues left around the house to help children find them. Sinterklaas and Black Peter preside over all these festivities and spread good cheer and happiness.

POLAND

hristmas in Poland is officially called *Bozz Narodzenie,* but more commonly it is known as *Gwiazdka,* or "little star." Consequently, the Poles use star decorations on just about everything during the Christmas season. Traditionally the stars were made of straw or goose feathers fastened together with candle wax.

The most important part of the Polish Christmas season comes during the celebration of the *Wigilia,* wherein each family gathers for a traditional supper. This occurs when the first star appears in the sky on Christmas Eve. The head of the household, usually a father or grandfather, takes holly bread, pronounces words of love and sharing, and then breaks and distributes the bread to all participants.

On January 6, the Poles celebrate the traditional date for the visit of the three wise men to the infant Jesus in Bethlehem. Groups of boys dress up as the wise men and other biblical figures. Just as in Sweden, they go from house to house carrying a long pole with a paper star at the top. For this reason, they are called Star Boys. In the star a candle burns. The Star Boys sing Christmas carols and perform short plays and other entertainments. For these efforts, they are given gifts of sweets and coins.

St. Nicholas is a very popular figure in Poland. He acts largely in his traditional religious roles as protector and patron saint, but he also encourages Polish children to behave well so that they will receive many gifts.

USA: 1863

anta Claus was born in the United States. In the 1860s he was still young, although he already looked old with his white beard and heavy stomach. Santa Claus got his name from the Dutch word for Saint Nicholas, "Sintaklaas."

Although the first Dutch settlers of New York did bring Sintaklaas with them from Holland in the 17th century, he did not become an important person at Christmas time until the American novelist Washington Irving put him in a novel that was written in 1809. This first Santa Claus was still called St. Nicholas. He smoked a pipe, and he flew about in a wagon without any reindeer. He did not yet have a red suit, nor did he live at the North Pole. But he did bring presents to children every year.

By 1863, Santa Claus finally had his own name and most of the traits that we now connect with him. It was in the 1860s that the American artist Thomas Nast began to draw a series of Christmas portraits of Santa Claus. Nast had been born and raised in Germany, so many of the German and Scandinavian customs that he knew as a boy were incorporated into his drawings of Santa and became American customs too. In Nast's drawings, Santa Claus wore a big red suit with fur trim around the wrists and neck. His black shoes had big buckles. He tried to stay hidden from most people, and he crawled down chimneys to bring gifts to children. But Santa Claus also smoked a long pipe and often wore holly leaves on his head in the 1860s. And his sleigh had only eight reindeer.

USA: MODERN

The modern American Santa Claus has become very important during Christmas to many children of the world. Santa Claus now has an appearance that almost everyone recognizes. His clothes are red, his belt and boots are black, and his head is covered by a soft red cap. Our modern Santa Claus also has a very familiar personality. Today, the American Santa Claus has a jolly countenance and a laugh to match. Santa Claus does not chuckle, he does not snicker. He boldly bellows, "Ho, Ho, Ho!"

Today, Santa Claus has a rather big "family," from his wife Mrs. Claus and the many elves that make toys, to the flying reindeer that pull his sleigh—including Rudolph, the Red-Nosed Reindeer, who guides Santa and the other reindeer through any kind of weather so that he can deliver gifts to the good children of the world. Santa Claus also has a very specific address at the North Pole. He still hauls huge bags of gifts down chimneys, and he still wonders if children have been naughty or nice. But now, many books and songs feature Santa Claus. He is even a television star.

Santa Claus has become one of the kindest and most charitable figures in American society. In the 20th century, American culture has influenced very many societies around the world. The result is that many traditional gift-givers, like Father Christmas in England and Julesvenn in Norway, have begun to resemble the modern American Santa Claus.

IRELAND

The Irish have embraced the tradition of Santa Claus almost as much as the people of the United States. There have always been very close familial and cultural ties between Ireland and the United States since the mid-19th century. This closeness ensured that beliefs about Santa Claus would be very similar in these two lands.

In Ireland, Santa Claus wears a red and white suit. His reindeer pull him through the winter sky, and children look forward to seeing him at the Christmas holiday more than they anticipate any other time of the year. Holly branches, with their unique leaves and berries, are brought into Irish homes, where they decorate windows and picture frames. Candles are lit in each window. On Christmas morning, children try to find the gifts that Santa Claus has hidden throughout the house.

Santa Claus is the main gift-giver in Ireland, but a few older traditions add to the modern Christmas celebrations. As they have for centuries, the Wren Boys come out on St. Stephen's Day, December 26. Originally they carried a long pole with a captive wren in a cage at the very top. These days, they are not likely to carry a real wren in the cage, but they still sing and go from house to house looking for gifts of money that will "free the wren."

NEW ZEALAND

he most unusual thing about Santa Claus in New Zealand is that he comes in the middle of the summer. Since New Zealand is an island country that is located below the Equator in the world's southern hemisphere, December falls during the summer months, just when students are finishing up their school year and looking forward to their summer vacations.

The Christmas traditions of New Zealand have come mostly from the English settlers who began arriving in New Zealand in the late 18th century. These settlers brought Father Christmas and other Christmas beliefs with them. This means that most New Zealanders saw Father Christmas as a tall man with long robes and perhaps sprigs of holly and mistletoe in his long white hair. The children of New Zealand have always hung stockings by the fire and hoped that Father Christmas would fill them with gifts and sweets.

In the last 20 or 30 years, ideas about Father Christmas have been changing. New Zealanders now talk about Santa Claus, and they think of him much like someone from the United States or Ireland would. It is now mostly older people who speak about Father Christmas. This is not the only influence that is working to change the Christmas traditions of New Zealand, however. Another force of change is the culture of the Maori people. This culture is very old, and the Maori people lived on the island of New Zealand long before the English settlers arrived. The spirits and creatures of their culture resemble the elves and gnomes of European Christmas traditions. In New Zealand, Santa Claus might soon acquire companions of Maori origin.

CANADA

anadian traditions about Santa Claus reflect a mingling of many different traditions. Since many Canadians are of French or English origin, they share the views of Santa Claus that are common in those countries.

Originally, Christmas celebrations in Canada were organized around the Twelve Days of Christmas and involved fancy foods and sporting competitions. Increasingly, though, Canadian Christmas traditions have become less religious in tone. One result is that their Santa figures have begun to resemble the American Santa Claus. English-speaking Canadians still think of Father Christmas, who brings brightly colored presents to eager children. Canadian children also continue to write letters to Father Christmas, which are thrown into the fireplace and "delivered" up the chimney. Children also hang stockings near the fireplace to "catch" Father Christmas's loose change.

A large number of Canadians speak French, and they inherited the Christmas traditions that are particular to France. A happy Père Noël makes his appearance on Christmas Eve, bringing gifts for all good children. There is also the companion of Père Noël, Père Fouchette, who carries a branch to punish the children who do not deserve the nice presents that Père Noël brings.

The cold climate of Canada is particularly good for making newer ideas about Santa Claus more appealing to Canadians. The concept of Santa Claus in a sleigh pulled by reindeer, who flies around the world from his home in the snow-covered North Pole, is gaining acceptance among the Canadian people.

SPAIN

pain is one of the countries that traditionally does not recognize Santa Claus as a jolly red-suited man who bears gifts. But Spanish children do look forward to gifts during the holidays. The Christmas season is celebrated with several religious festivals that have been part of the Spanish Christmas tradition for hundreds of years. These celebrations are the Feast of the Immaculate Conception, which begins on December 8; the Feast of the Holy Innocents on December 28; and the Feast of the Epiphany, which begins on January 6.

Spanish Christmas celebrations are deeply religious holidays, and they are influenced by the sincere piety of the Spanish people. One of the most important stories in the Christian story of Jesus is his birth in Bethlehem. This story tells of wise men who travelled from far in the East, guided by a star, to see the birth of Jesus. These wise men brought gifts. Spanish children look forward to the coming of the Three Wise Men on Epiphany Eve. Children put their shoes on their windowsills. They fill them with carrots, straw and barley to feed the horses or donkeys of the Wise Men. The children especially hope to receive a visit from the wise man Balthazar, who usually rides a donkey, and, more importantly, is the wise man that they believe leaves all the gifts. In the morning, the carrots and straw will be gone and many gifts will fill the shoes.

PORTUGAL

n Portugal, the gift-giving tradition was defined mostly by the strong Christian religious beliefs of the people. Portuguese children await the coming of the Three Wise Men during Christmas time. On Epiphany Eve, January 5, children put all their shoes along windowsills and doorways and fill them with carrots and straw. They hope to lure the wise men's horses to their houses during the night and hope to find their shoes packed with gifts and treats in the morning. In the Mediterranean climate of Portugal, these treats are mostly candied fruits and sweet breads.

As with the Spanish people, the Portuguese traditionally do not recognize a red-suited Santa Claus as the person who brings Christmas gifts. Nevertheless, gifts are a big part of the many Christmas celebrations of Portugal. The Christmas Feast of the Immaculate Conception and the Feast of the Holy Innocents both involve the sharing of gifts.

The Portuguese have had their own Christmas feast for many centuries. This feast is the *consoada,* which takes place in the early morning of Christmas Day. The Portuguese set extra places at the table for the souls of the dead. They give a gift of food to these souls and hope that by doing so the fortunes of the next year will be good.

MEXICO

exico shares many Christmas traditions with Spain. Mexicans call their main Christmas celebration *La Posada,* which is a religious procession that reenacts the search for shelter by Joseph and Mary before Jesus was born. During this procession, celebrants go from house to house carrying the images of Joseph and Mary and looking for shelter.

Santa Claus is not a prominent figure in these festivities, but the bright red of his suit is represented in the traditional flower of the Mexican Christmas season. This flower is the poinsettia, which has a brilliant red star-shaped bloom. It is believed that a little boy was walking to church to see a beautiful Christmas nativity scene that showed the birth of Jesus. He realized before he arrived that he had nothing to offer the Christ Child, so he gathered up some plain green branches that he saw at the side of the road. When he brought the branches to the church, his friends laughed and made fun of him. But when the little boy laid them near the manger, they bloomed with a bright red poinsettia flower on each branch.

Mexican children also receive many gifts. On Christmas day, the children are blindfolded and take turns trying to break a decorated clay piñata that dangles and swings at the end of a rope. When the piñata is broken, all the children who have been waiting anxiously nearby dive madly to recover the candy that was stored inside. As in Spain, good Mexican children also receive gifts on January 6 from the Three Wise Men.

ITALY

taly has Christmas traditions that are similar to those of Spain and Portugal. Christmas is a sacred holiday that is observed with solemn ceremonies and a Midnight Mass in churches. Italians exchange gifts on January 6, the Christian Feast of the Epiphany.

It is not, however, the Three Wise Men who bring presents, as in Spain, but La Befana. According to legend, the three wise men stopped on their long journey to Bethlehem. They asked an old woman for food to eat and shelter in which to rest themselves before they continued their journey. But the old woman refused because she was too busy with her housework. So the wise men went on their way, both tired and hungry. A few hours later, the old woman had a change of heart. She tried to find the wise men but could not. The old woman is now called La Befana, which means Epiphany. She roams the earth searching for the Christ Child and carries presents in her apron. She wishes to make amends for turning away the wise men who were traveling to see the baby Jesus. This is why, dressed as a fairy queen, La Befana brings gifts to good children. Unfortunately, La Befana also brings bags of ashes for bad children, and then she is depicted as an old witch.

In Italy there is a whole day that is devoted to this woman. This is Befana Day, which falls on January 6. Befana Day is a day of fairs all over the country, especially in the capital, Rome.

anta Claus exists in many different parts of Asia, although he has different names and different appearances. Christian children in China decorate trees with colorful ornaments. These ornaments are made of folded paper and resemble chains, flowers, and lanterns. The children also hang muslin stockings and hope that "Christmas Old Man" will fill them with gifts and treats.

The non-Christian people of China, who are much more numerous, also celebrate the Christmas season. They call this season the "Spring Festival" and celebrate with many festivities that include delicious meals and the veneration of ancestors. During these celebrations, children are the main focus of their caring parents, just as children are the focus of Santa Claus in other cultures. Chinese children receive new clothes and toys, eat delicious food, and watch firecracker displays.

Customs are different in other parts of Asia. In India, for example, Christians will decorate banana or mango trees, since India is a tropical country. They will also light small oil-burning lamps as Christmas decorations and fill their churches with red flowers. Indians will also give gifts to family members and baksheesh, or charity, to the impoverished people of the country. In Japan, Santa Claus is represented by a god or priest named Hoteiosho. He is always pictured as a kindly old man who roams about with a huge pack slung behind him. Hoteiosho is believed to have eyes in the back of his head so that he can see children who misbehave.

ENGLAND

nglish children know Santa Claus by the name "Father Christmas." Traditionally, Father Christmas was usually portrayed with long flowing robes of green or scarlet and sprigs of holly and mistletoe stuck in his long white hair. He may also appear as a giant who carries a yule log or bowl of Christmas punch.

Father Christmas today looks much like an American Santa Claus, but he is still often associated with the ancient gods Saturn and Odin. English children write letters to Father Christmas and ask him for toys and other gifts, but they do not mail them in the usual way. Instead, they toss the letters into the fireplace, where the draft of air carries the letters up the chimney to the realm of Father Christmas. At least this is what children hope, for if the letter is not carried up the chimney, then their wishes can not be fulfilled. Hopefully, Father Christmas will see these smoky messages and bring many gifts to be opened on Christmas afternoon.

It is due to Father Christmas that we hang stockings by the fireplace. He once dropped some gold coins while he was coming down the chimney. English fireplaces are big and usually filled with ashes. If anything were to drop into these ashes, then they would be completely lost. Fortunately, some stockings had been hung up to dry in the fire's heat, and they caught the loose coins. If most people now do not hang up stockings to catch Father Christmas's lost change, they do hope to find many gifts filling them all the same.

SCOTLAND

In Scotland, the religious beliefs of the people have largely prevented the survival of a Christmas tradition. In the Middle Ages, the Scots did celebrate a great festival at Christmas time. This festival was dominated by a person called the "Abbot of Unreason." He dressed in clerical robes and supervised the celebrations. Unfortunately, the Abbot of Unreason often became unruly and was finally banned in the 16th century.

The Scottish people celebrate Christmas in a rather somber way today, but they celebrate New Year's Eve with great enthusiasm. They call New Year's Eve "Hogmanay," which is a word that may derive from a special cake that was traditionally given to children on that day. The Scots have a New Year's tradition that is similar to some English Christmas traditions. It is called "first-footing" and is a ritual that foretells good luck during the following year. The first-footer is the first person to step into a house in the new year. The first-footer can bring good fortune to the home depending on his or her hair color. Often the first-footer is given treats and gifts to ensure this good fortune. A popular first-footing carol reveals some of the gifts that might be brought:

> *I wish you a merry Christmas*
> *And a happy New Year;*
> *A pocket full of money*
> *And a cellar full of beer,*
> *And a great fat pig*
> *To last you all the year.*

In Scotland, Santa Claus would probably be considered a first-rate first-footer.

CHRONOLOGY

0 A.D. Jesus Christ is born in Bethlehem

280 Birth of St. Nicholas of Myra in Patara (Turkey)

353 The feast of Christ's birth is set on December 25

750 The first Christmas Tree is decorated in Austria

1224 The crèche is created by St. Francis and becomes popular in France

1680 Dutch settlers bring "Sintaklaas" to New Amsterdam (later New York City)

1790 English settlers bring Father Christmas to New Zealand

1809 Debut of Modern Santa Claus in Washington Irving's novel, *Diedrich Knickerbocker's A History of New York from the Beginning of the World to the End of the Dutch Dynasty*

1822 Dr. Clement Clarke Moore writes his poem, *A Visit from St. Nicholas*

1866 First drawings of Santa Claus by Thomas Nast in *Harper's Weekly* magazine

1917 Grandfather Frost and Babouschka take the place of St. Nicholas in Russia after the Revolution

1939 Rudolph the Red-Nosed Reindeer makes his debut in advertising posters for Montgomery Wards stores

1947 A famous American movie, *Miracle on 34th Street,* included a main character named Kris Kringle, thus linking this name for the Christkind with Santa Claus

INDEX

FURTHER READING

Chris, Teresa. *The Story of Santa Claus.* London: Apple Press, 1992.

Nissenbaum, Stephen. *The Mythmaking Frame of Mind: Social Imagination and American Culture,* James Gilbert, et al., eds. Belmont, Calif.: Watson Publishing, 1992.

Restad, Penne L. *Christmas in America: A History.* New York: Oxford University Press, 1995.

Siefker, Phyllis. *Santa Claus, Last of the Wild Men: The Origins and Evolution of Saint Nicholas, Spanning 50,000 Years.* Jefferson, N.C.: McFarland, 1997.